D0605370

Workers
YOU Know

Carpenter

Workers YOU Know

Carpenter

Angela McHaney Brown

RAINTREE
STECK-VAUGHN
PUBLISHERS
RSVP

A Harcourt Company

Austin   New York
www.steck-vaughn.com

Published by Raintree Steck-Vaughn Publishers,
an imprint of Steck-Vaughn Company

Art Director: Max Brinkmann
Editor: Pam Wells
Design and Illustration: Proof Positive/Farrowlyne Associates, Inc.
Planned and Produced by
Proof Positive/Farrowlyne Associates, Inc.

Library of Congress Cataloging-in-Publication Data
Brown, Angela McHaney
 Carpenter/Angela McHaney Brown.
  p. cm. — (Workers you know)
 Summary: A carpenter describes the many aspects of her job and the training and skills needed in this profession.
 ISBN 0-8172-5596-6
  1. Carpentry—Vocational guidance—Juvenile literature. 2. Carpenters—Juvenile literature. [1. Carpentry. 2. Carpenters. 3. Occupations.] I. Title. II. Series.

TH5608.7 .B726 2000
694'.023—dc21
                                                                             99–057363

Printed and bound in the United States
1 2 3 4 5 6 7 8 9 0 LB 03 02 01 00

Note: You will find more information about becoming a carpenter on the last page of this book.

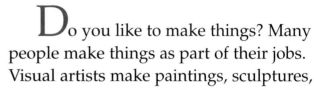

Do you like to make things? Many people make things as part of their jobs. Visual artists make paintings, sculptures, stained glass, and other works of art. Mechanics build automobile engines. Tool-and-die makers make tools that are used to cut and form metal. Some people make shoes, clothing, and even dishes as part of their jobs.

I make things, too. I am a carpenter. My name is Jenny Rasmussen.

Carpenters build furniture, houses, buildings, and many other things. Most carpenters build things out of wood. But some carpenters also build things out of metal or plastic.

I'm going to build another room onto the Jordans' house because the Jordans are going to have a baby soon. Their family is going to be bigger, so they need their house to be bigger, too.

One week ago, the Jordans had a family meeting. They talked about how they wanted their new room to look. Then they drew a picture of the new room.

This is the Jordans' picture. The numbers on the sides show how tall and how wide they want the room to be. The Jordans drew a window and a door. They even drew a special place for a fish tank.

The picture the Jordans drew gave me a lot of information, but not enough to start building. I sent them to see my friend Sharon. Sharon is an architect, someone who designs buildings and rooms. Architects draw up plans, detailed pictures of the buildings and rooms called blueprints.

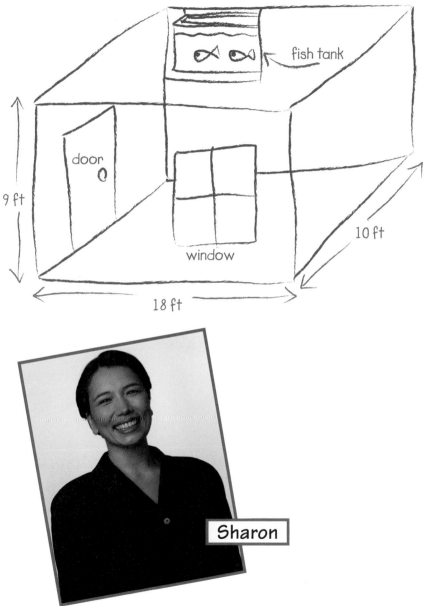

fish tank

door

9 ft

window

10 ft

18 ft

Sharon

Sharon used a computer to draw the blueprints of the Jordans' new room. The blueprints showed all the same information that was on the Jordans' drawing. But Sharon added some other information. Her plans showed how the room will be heated and where the outlets for the electricity will go.

The architect made sure that the plans followed all of the city's safety laws. For example, the laws in our city say that bedrooms must have two exits that can be used in case of a fire. One exit can be a window. The Jordans' new room will have two windows and a door, so it follows the city's rules.

Carpenters need good math skills. They also need to be able to explain things clearly. After Sharon finished the blueprints, I talked about the project with the Jordans. I told them how much I thought the room would cost. Then, I showed them how I added the cost of the materials to the cost of the labor— my pay and the other workers' pay.

I also told the Jordans how long it would take to build the new room. I warned them that it might take longer if we had bad weather. The Jordans asked a lot of questions, and I answered all of them carefully.

materials + labor = total cost

Before I start a big job, I always study my blueprints. I make a list of the materials I will need. I don't want to waste money buying more wood than I need, but I also don't want to waste time going back to the lumberyard for more if I run out. I want to buy just the right amount.

The blueprints tell me how big the room will be on the inside, and how big it will be on the outside. They tell me where the windows and door will go, and how big each will be. From these plans, I will learn the shape of the roof and how high it will be. This roof will have sloping sides that make a triangle, so snow will slide off of it in the winter.

The blueprints also show in which wall the heating duct will go, and how much space it will take. A heating duct is a metal pipe that will carry warm air from the Jordans' furnace to the baby's room. I will have to include space in the wall for a heating vent. The vent is the place where the warm air will come out of the duct. The blueprints tell everything about the room—even where the electrical outlets and the overhead light will go.

A blueprint shows every part that goes into a building. It also shows the exact size of every part. Just as you read a book, carpenters read blueprints. We use blueprints to guide us as we work.

warm air

I start work bright and early, at 7:30 in the morning. But I'm not ready to start building yet! The first thing I do is to show Bradley and Lamont, the concrete workers, where to pour the cement for the room's foundation. The cement foundation will give me a smooth, flat surface to build the room on. It will also help to keep the room from settling down into the ground.

While the cement is drying, I drive over to the lumberyard. The lumberyard has many different types of wood. I love the smell and the feel of wood. I guess that's why I became a carpenter.

12

Choosing the right kind of wood is important. Hardwoods like oak, walnut, and maple are good for building furniture. Softwoods like pine, fir, and redwood are good for building houses. You have to understand some science to choose wood for a project. Some kinds of wood split and crack easily. Others get warped, or bent, when they stand in rain or humid weather. I like to use spruce, because it's strong and doesn't warp easily.

When I buy wood, I check each board to make sure it isn't split, warped, or crooked. When I'm satisfied, I pay for the wood and load it into my truck. My next stop is the hardware store.

Whew! It's a good thing I'm strong. These boxes of nails weigh 50 pounds each! Let's see. . . . I have my wood, nails, screws, and my box of tools. I think I need a bigger truck! I'll tie the materials down with bungee cords to make sure they don't fall out. Then I'll drive back to the Jordans' to start working!

First, I unload my materials and get them organized. If my materials are organized, the work will go faster when I start to build. The foundation is dry now, so I use a tape measure and chalk to mark where each wall will go. I arrange my materials in piles, next to each place where I will need them. I also unpack my tools.

Of course, my two most important tools are the ones I use all the time—my hands. I wear thick gloves to protect them while I work. I also wear special boots to protect my feet in case I drop something. The toes of my boots are lined with steel!

When I finally start building, the first thing I do is make the frame—the skeleton for the room. Whether it is a glass dome or a nomad's hut, a frame holds a building together.

As part of the frame, I lay down big, strong pieces of wood, or joists (joysts). These joists are also called 2 x 10s, because they are two inches thick and ten inches wide. On top of the 2 x 10s, I build a subfloor, the area under the room's floor, out of 3/4-inch thick plywood. Later, workers will put in carpeting, tile, or a hardwood floor.

How do you think I attach these pieces of wood? I do it the old fashioned way—with a hammer and nails! Hammering is harder than it looks. You have to be especially careful with fine woods not to split the wood with the nail. If the wood splits, the nail will not be able to hold it together.

To avoid splitting the wood, I sometimes drill a hole first, with my power drill. Then, I hold the nail with my fingers and tap it into the hole with my hammer. That sets the nail in place, so I don't have to hold it with my fingers anymore. Finally, I take my hand away from the nail and hammer the nail into the wood. Did you know that you should use your whole arm to hammer a nail? Some people just swing their arms from the elbow, but your arm gets tired faster if you hammer that way.

17

Part of my job is checking my work. I check carefully as I go along. If I don't check my work during the job, I might have to tear down the whole room and start over because of one mistake!

One tool I always use is a level. It has a small glass tube with an air bubble inside that tells me if the piece of wood is straight. When the wood is straight, the air bubble sits between two lines on the tube.

I also use math to check my work. To make sure a corner is square, I make a triangle. I start in the corner and mark a point three feet from it on one side. Next, I mark four feet from the corner on the other side. Finally, I measure the distance between the two marks—the third side of the triangle. If it measures five feet, I know the corner is square.

5 ft.

4 ft.

3 ft.

Greg

Building a room takes a lot of work. I'm glad Greg is helping me. Greg is an apprentice. An apprentice is a beginner who works with a more experienced worker to learn how to do a job. I used to be an apprentice, but now I have experience.

During this project, I am teaching Greg how to lay out a building, how to build a frame, and how to finish the job. But Greg also takes classes to learn how to do these things. He's been my apprentice for more than three years now. Greg has learned so much that he is almost a master carpenter himself.

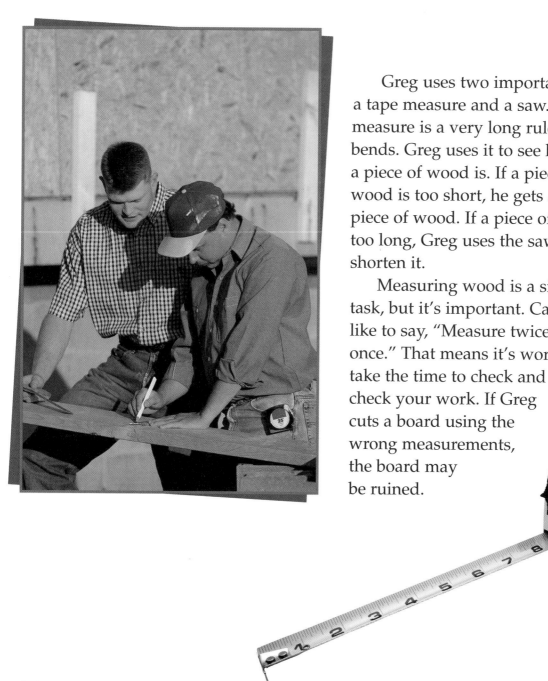

Greg uses two important tools—a tape measure and a saw. The tape measure is a very long ruler that bends. Greg uses it to see how long a piece of wood is. If a piece of wood is too short, he gets a longer piece of wood. If a piece of wood is too long, Greg uses the saw to shorten it.

Measuring wood is a simple task, but it's important. Carpenters like to say, "Measure twice, cut once." That means it's worth it to take the time to check and double-check your work. If Greg cuts a board using the wrong measurements, the board may be ruined.

Carpenters use a lot of numbers in their work. We are always measuring and doing addition and subtraction. For example, Greg needs a piece of wood that is 29 inches long.

If the piece of wood he has is 52 inches long, how much wood does he need to cut off? That's right, he has to cut off 23 inches.

Greg and I need to be careful when we use our tools. For example, a power saw makes lots of sawdust when it cuts wood. We wear safety goggles to protect our eyes from the dust when we use the power saw. We also wear a dust mask to keep from breathing in the dust.

CAUTION: Never use a power tool without an adult present.

Brenda is also working on the Jordans' new room. She is an electrician. She connects lights, switches, and power outlets in buildings. Carpenters work with electricians, plumbers, and other workers to build houses. We all get to do what we do best.

The electrician has to do her work before we can finish building the walls for the new room. That's because the electric cables have to go inside the walls. Like carpenters, electricians use special tools. Brenda uses a screwdriver and pliers.

Brenda

CAUTION: Electricity is very dangerous. Even electricity coming out of an outlet can hurt you.

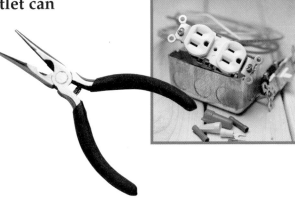

23

Electrical cables are not the only things that have to go inside the walls. Jack is putting up sheets of insulation (in-se-**lay**-shun) to help keep the room warm in winter. How does the insulation do that? It's a matter of science.

Some materials, like the metal in pots and pans, conduct, or carry, heat very well. If your house were made of metal, the metal would cause heat to be lost to the outside. Without insulation, you would be cold in winter—just the opposite of what you want to be. Insulation acts like a blanket for your house. It keeps the heat inside.

Did you notice the openings I left in the room's frame? Two of these openings will be windows. Each window unit consists of panes of glass and a sash, the framework that holds the window in place.

Now, I'm ready to put the windows in the room frame. After the windows are in place, I make sure they are straight up and down as well as across. Then I add small pieces of wood, called shims (shimz), to fill in the cracks between the window frames and the house frame. I hammer in nails to keep the windows in place. Finally, I use caulk (cawk), a material to seal the window in place and make it waterproof.

I'm eager to finish building this room, but one more thing has to happen first. Bruce works for the city. He is an inspector. Before we finish the walls, Bruce has to check them. He makes sure that the electrical wiring is safe and that the frame is strong and sturdy. Bruce uses a tape measure to check distances. He'll check to make sure the frame is square and level, just the way I did. He'll also use special tools to make sure the frame is strong enough. Bruce takes notes as he works.

I always feel a little nervous watching Bruce inspect my work. I know I did a good job. But if he finds a problem, Greg and I have to fix it, or the city will order us to stop working on the room. I wouldn't want that to happen!

Bruce

Back to work at last! After the frame is finished, I nail drywall onto it. Drywall is a hard covering I use to finish walls and ceilings. Drywall is strong, like cement. But it is also easy to cut, like wood.

This part of the job is where I really need someone to help me. Drywall comes in big sheets that are awkward to carry. We will have to measure the drywall very carefully before we cut it. We have to make sure that the edge of each piece of drywall will be next to a piece of wood in the frame, so we have something to nail the drywall to. After we nail the drywall to the frame, we tape all the edges together. That gives the wall a smoother surface. But we will sand and plaster the drywall to make it even smoother.

Carpenter

Do you remember the Jordans' drawing? This is the space they wanted us to build for a big fish tank. Tony from the pet store is going to build the fish tank. Janet Jordan is helping Tony measure the space. She wants to be sure the new tank fits perfectly.

Tony

Being a carpenter takes more than strength. It also takes a good sense of balance! Greg and I are always very careful when we build roofs. We built the frame for the roof using rafters (**raf**-terz), strong pieces of wood that support the roof. This roof forms a triangle with the room's ceiling. Greg and I used math to figure out the exact angle to place the rafters at.

After we built the frame, we nailed plywood to the roof. Now, we are covering it with roofing felt and shingles. The shingles (**shing**-gulz) are thin squares of material that are laid in rows so that each shingle covers part of the shingles put down before. The roofing felt and shingles will keep water from leaking into the new room for the baby.

Carpenter

Carpenters use special pieces of wood to make their work more beautiful. Greg puts trim around the doors and windows. I put siding on the outside of the room. On big buildings, carpenters work in teams. Some of the carpenters build the frame. The rest of the carpenters put on the trim and siding.

When Greg and I finish our work, other workers will come and put the finishing touches on the room. Painters will paint the walls. Paint not only protects walls, but it also decorates them. A carpet service person will measure the floor and lay down wall-to-wall carpet. The Jordans have chosen a soft carpet for the baby to crawl on.

My work on the new room is finally done! Janet is eager to have all the decorating finished. Then, she will put the fish into the tank.

I will see a lot of fish on my next job. I am going to build a dock for boats! I'll get more than my feet wet on that job. I am going to need some help, too. Would you like to be my new apprentice?

For Information About Becoming a Carpenter, Contact:
Associated Builders and Contractors
1300 North 17th Street
Rosslyn, VA 22209

Associated General Contractors of America, Inc.
333 John Carlyle Street
Suite 200
Alexandria, VA 22314

Carpenter Training, Education, and Requirements:
Some carpenters learn their trade through an apprenticeship program that combines on-the-job training with formal classes. Others learn their trade informally on the job without any classroom instruction. Apprenticeships are offered by local chapters of unions such as the ones listed above. To be accepted as an apprentice, applicants must be at least 17 years old and may have to pass an entrance exam. Apprenticeship programs last 3–4 years and include classes in structural design, layout, form building, framing, finishing, mathematics, first aid, safety, blueprint reading, and freehand sketching.

Related Careers:

Construction Manager	Architect
Plumber	Electrician
Building Inspector	Roofer